Ghost Story PLOT SKELETONS

Writing Exciting Ghost Stories : Age 9 Plus

By Alan Peat and Julie Barnfather

Illustrated by Glyn Matthews

PUBLISHED BY: Creative Educational Press Ltd
2 The Walled Garden
Grange Park Drive
Biddulph
ST8 7TA

Tel: 07789938923
Fax: 01782 379398

PRINTED BY: York Publishing Services Ltd., 64, Hallfield Road, Layerthorpe, York, YO31 7ZQ

Alan Peat   www.alanpeat.com

info@alanpeat.com

Glyn Matthews   www.glyn-matthews.co.uk

glynmatthews@btinternet.com

ISBN: 978-0-9544755-2-9

Also available from Creative Educational Press Ltd:
Improving Narrative Writing: Thinkabout Pupil Self-Assessment (co-author Barry Silsby)

Other titles by Alan Peat available through Creative Educational Press Ltd (www.alanpeat.com)

Key Stage 1 Poetry Pack (Questions Publishing)
Key Stage 2 Poetry Pack (Questions Publishing)
Word Games at Key Stage 2 (Nash Pollock Publishing)
Improving Story Writing KS 1 &2 (Nash Pollock Publishing)
Improving Non-Fiction Writing KS 1 & 2 (co-written with Margaret McNeil)
(Nash Pollock Publishing)

Design: Julie Barnfather
Cover design: Simon Matthews
Additional design: Christopher Storey

CONTENTS

ACKNOWLEDGEMENTS

Many thanks to Suki Powar, Headteacher, and Nicola Floyd, Year Six teacher, at Hazel Slade Primary School, Staffordshire.

And special thanks to Year Six:

Michael Barrett, Joe Bishop, Robbie Bradley, Gemma-Lee Campbell, Harriet Dawson, Samuel Elstone, Jessica England, Samuel Fletcher, James Hardwick, Charlotte Harper, Ryan Harvey, William Henderson, Daniel Holmes, Amber-Louise Ingram, Asa Jones, Chelsea Jones, Danielle Jones, Neeve Macdonald, Jack Maddox, David Mair, Joe Mann, Emma Mcallister, Emily Morris, Jack Mucklow, Samuel Phillips, Amelia Quigley, Ryan Rogers-Hinks, Leanne Shepherdson, Daniella Spittle, Andrew Sutton, Emily Walker, Charlotte Whitehouse, Jason Wilson and Bethanie Wright.

Thanks also to Alan Peat Snr.... and lastly, but not least, to Glyn Matthews, who knew what we wanted even when we didn't!

Alan Peat and Julie Barnfather

INTRODUCTION

'Ghost Story Plot Skeletons' is the first in a series of books which will cover the whole range of narrative genres, including myths and legends, fairy tales, science fiction etc.

They have been designed to complement the 'blocked units' in the 2007 Literacy Framework (UK), specifically *Stories with historical settings* and *Stories with familiar locations.*

The idea originated when the authors became aware that many pupils could not 'hold' a whole story together. Although they could start adequately and produce effective characterisations or descriptive pieces, structure often disintegrated thereafter. Their stories often became lists of the main character's actions: "And then he did X. And then he did Y." etc.
While the children knew they were expected to continue writing, they had little idea of how to sustain any sense of dynamic within whole stories. The pupils themselves were also painfully aware that they had not produced effective stories.

Assuming the child's perspective, we believe it is better to **succeed** in expanding the elements of a given plot skeleton than to **fail** at the writing of a whole story when no plot skeleton is provided. The major benefit of our approach is that it develops pupils' belief in their own writing abilities.

With this in mind, we have sought to develop Alan Peat's concept of 'plot skeletons' (first published in *IMPROVING LITERACY: CREATIVE APPROACHES* *Improving Story Writing at Key Stage 1 and 2*, Nash Pollock Publishing 2002) as a means of supporting pupils' understanding of plot structure across the narrative genres. Teachers may also find Alan's Boxing Clever game, from the same book, useful for children who are struggling to retain story structure. This approach has been used with significant success in hundreds of school across the UK. More details of this and other of Alan's techniques can be found at: www.alanpeat.com

What is a Plot Skeleton?

A plot skeleton is, quite simply, the 'bare bones' of a story. We have broken down story plot structures into sequential, numbered elements. In this book there are between eight and twenty elements in each plot skeleton and there are twenty-five skeletons in total.

Plot skeletons provide children with organisational support. The entire structure of each ghost story is provided within the plot skeletons. As a result, pupils can concentrate on 'composition and effect': making their writing exciting! For reluctant writers of all ages, the plot skeleton is less threatening than a blank sheet of paper.

Plot skeletons:
- make whole story structures clear
- 'chunk' success into achievable, manageable elements
- appeal to children who are predominantly 'mathematical-logical', i.e. those who prefer maths to literacy. (By breaking down the story writing process into a series of sequenced, numbered elements, the teacher creates a structure which motivates these children.)

On page 17, we have also included suggestions for 'further reading', making links where we can between our plot skeletons and stories written by published authors. We strongly believe that the reading of effective and enjoyable stories helps to engender a positive writing culture within a school. If plot skeletons are used in this context children will have many opportunities to compare, contrast, discuss, criticise and learn from other writers.

HOW TO USE PLOT SKELETONS

We have suggested two teaching sequences (pupils **are** more likely to develop embedded understanding if BOTH sequences are used.)
Teachers will, however, develop and adapt these sequences in their own ways; this is exactly what we would hope for! An account of how one teacher adapted Plot Skeletons for use in her classroom is included as Appendix 1 (page 71).

Teaching Sequence 1: Deconstruction

The teacher reads an entire ghost story to the class/group. Many superb ghost stories exist and it is best to choose an example which the teacher finds exciting. The teacher models how to reduce the tale to its essential components – the plot skeleton. This process is essentially one of isolating the 'main parts' of the story.
We suggest that teachers model this for the first part (no more than a quarter) of the story, after which the pupils, in groups, complete the process. One pupil in each group acts as scribe and the pupil-produced plot skeletons are then shared and discussed.
This process of deconstructing a story to produce a plot-skeleton helps pupils to understand how the skeletons work.

Teaching Sequence 2: Reconstruction

The second teaching sequence is a reconstruction. Initially, pupils are divided into groups of between four and six. Each group is given a copy of the same plot skeleton photocopied from this book. The teacher then explains that each group is going to **turn the plot skeleton into a finished story** or **bring the skeleton to life!**
The first numbered element is fleshed out (with the teacher acting as scribe) as a model of how to proceed thereafter.

e.g. From Plot Skeleton 1- Lovers Parted By Death

1. A house has a reputation for being haunted – strange things happen there.

In order to extend this into one or more paragraphs, the teacher models the process of adding details through structured class/group questioning, using as starting points the prompt symbols included in each skeleton. The prompt symbols at the end of the sentences act as visual reminders of a broad range of writing techniques pupils may wish to use in their writing.

Although the symbols act as a prompt...

👁 locational writing – describe what you can see

... pupils should be taught that they do <u>not</u> have to follow the prompt. They are guides rather than requirements. We include them as they encourage pupils to, at least, consider a broad range of authorial techniques. They could also be used as a form of criteria based self-assessment.
We have linked our prompt symbols to the Key Stage 2 SAT 5 Band mark scheme introduced in the UK in 2003. All of the prompt symbols used in the book are explained on the following page.

SYMBOL KEY
Think about including ...

1   historical facts

2A   sentence with 2 adjectives before and after noun

!   a description of a character (include 'Show Not Tell')

   a list sentence

◀ ▶   O.I. sentence (outside inside—how a character appears on the outside but really feels on the inside)

👁   locational writing – describe what you can see

👂   locational writing – describe what you can hear

👃   locational writing – describe what you can smell

☁   locational writing – use weather to create 'mood'

☹ ☺   emotions – how characters are feeling

"🗣." Speech by one character ending with a full stop

"🗣!" Speech by one character ending with an
     exclamation mark

"🗣?" Speech by one character ending with a question mark

"👥." Speech between two or more characters ending with a full-stop

"👥!" Speech between two or more characters ending with an
     exclamation mark

"👥?" Speech between two or more characters ending with a question mark

PRODUCING EFFECTIVE NARRATIVE WRITING

Children can be taught a range of techniques to help them to write exciting stories.
Some of the following approaches, and many more, can be found in Alan's book *IMPROVING LITERACY: CREATIVE APPROACHES Improving Story Writing at Key Stage 1 and 2*, (Nash Pollock Publishing 2002). As the prompt symbols cross reference to some of these strategies, the following explanations have been included for ease of use.

Linking historical 'fact' and fiction to produce 'faction'

Prompt symbol used: $\boxed{1}$

Historical details ; facts about costume, domestic settings and lifestyles etc can be included in many of the plot skeletons in this book. In fact, most ghost stories can be set in any historical timeframe. If teachers wish to site the plot skeletons in a specific historic period, then the plots would remain the same, though the details would need to be modified; for example, a coach could replace the car in Plot Skeleton 2; the couple could be Victorians visiting a Roman site in Plot Skeleton 4 etc.
The resulting pieces of 'faction' have the added advantage of 'contextualising' history, whilst also embedding story structure through an area of the curriculum other than literacy.
We have directly linked **14** of our Ghost Story Plot Skeletons to History Units (UK). They are:

Unit	Plot Skeleton
6A Why have people invaded and settled in Britain in the past? A Roman Case study	4 11 22 23
8 What were the differences between the lives of rich and poor people in Tudor times?	3
9 What was it like for children in the Second World War?	7
11/12 What was it like for children living in Victorian Britain? How did life change in our locality in Victorian times?	1 3 4 5 6 8 9 11

2A sentences (2 adjectives before and after the noun)

Prompt symbol used: 2A
At certain appropriate points in the plot skeletons we have suggested that children use a "2A sentence".

'2A' is an abbreviation for "2 adjectives before the noun and 2 adjectives after the noun."
In a sense it is a less complex way of asking pupils to write "extended phrases both before and after the noun" (level 4 criteria). The simple name, 2A, makes this sentence type more memorable for pupils.

For example:

In Plot Skeleton 8—The Phantom Coach we suggest that pupils might include a 2A sentence in in their third element -

3. I knew I could not last the night out in the open and made my way towards a light, it was a house. I was given food, drink and shelter. $2A$

An appropriate 2A sentence for this might be:

It was a <u>dark</u> , <u>brooding</u> house with <u>black</u>, <u>filthy</u> windows.

The end result is more descriptive, evocative writing.

Exciting character descriptions—Show Not Tell

Prompt symbol used: ❗

Many children can, and will, happily produce a piece of visual-only character description. Of course, we want to know what a character is wearing (especially if it is a piece of historical costume description) and what he/she looks like etc. But we also want children to move beyond description of the visual by, for example, focussing on a character's actions as well as their appearance.   Children should therefore describe what a character <u>does</u> which reveals their emotional state, thereby affecting a story's mood and atmosphere.

The technique is called 'Show Not Tell' and is also explained in Alan's *IMPROVING LITERACY: CREATIVE APPROACHES Improving Story Writing at Key Stage 1 and 2*, (Nash Pollock Publishing 2002).

Try the following as a way of introducing this:

1.   The teacher chooses a word to describe an emotional state which is appropriate for a ghost story e.g. frightened/terrified/relieved.

The sentence: **He/she was frightened** is written on the board/whiteboard with the title:

A 'TELL' SENTENCE

2. The teacher then explains he/she is going to **SHOW** what a character does when he/she is feeling frightened. The teacher then 'acts out ' this emotion, while asking questions along the lines of:

"What's happening with my hands?

What are my legs doing?

What does my voice sound like?

What does my face look like?" etc

3. The title: **SHOW SENTENCES** is written on the board/whiteboard with the following beneath:

His hands …………………………………………………..

His legs …………………………………………………

His voice ………………………………………………..

His face ………………………………………………

4. Children are then asked to complete the sentences in the most effective way they can. If the **"More than one Word Answer"** rule is appplied (see page 13) then the sentences will be more powerful.

An example of 'Show Not Tell' characterisation is included below.

His heart stopped still for a second.

His whole body was shaking madly.

The room laughed at him as his mouth went dry.

His eyes were as wide as a mountain.

By Daniel and Jack, Hazel Slade Primary School

List sentences

Prompt symbol used: 🖺

A list sentence contains two or more adjectives before a noun, thereby creating a striking visual image in the reader's mind.

e.g.

One <u>bright,</u> <u>fresh,</u> <u>scented</u> morning a family of four set out on holiday in the countryside.

By Bethanie Wright and Gemma-Lee Campbell, Hazel Slade Primary School

It should be modelled with repeated emphasis on the inclusion of commas between and after the first two adjectives.

The teacher may wish to use a brainstorming activity when teaching 'list sentences', asking for suggestions from the class, modelling the sentence and perhaps replacing some earlier ideas with more powerful adjectives as they emerge.

In this instance the teacher **would** be asking pupils for single word answers.

However, the following activity suggests how phrase-banked, rather than single word, answers can be encouraged during the brainstorming process.

More effective brainstorming

Brainstorming is a useful class technique which encourages pupils to share ideas. When used in conjunction with the plot skeletons, the teacher begins by choosing one of the elements e.g.

PLOT SKELETON 1

A house has a reputation for being haunted – strange things happen there.

An important aspect of the sentence, such as 'haunted house' is written as the central focus of the brainstorm (as below). Pupils are then asked to suggest 'haunted house' ideas which are then incorporated in the brainstorm:

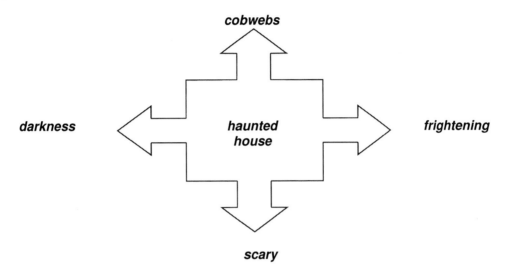

You will probably find, as we do, that pupils tend to offer single word answers rather than phrases – the above example is therefore typical. If the teachers wishes to raise the cognitive demand level of the lesson, then the '**More Than One Word Answer**' game can be played. The first time a pupil offers a single word answer, introduce the rule that each answer has to be longer than a single word. The end result provides a more useful visual learning referent which can be used by children to develop their stories:

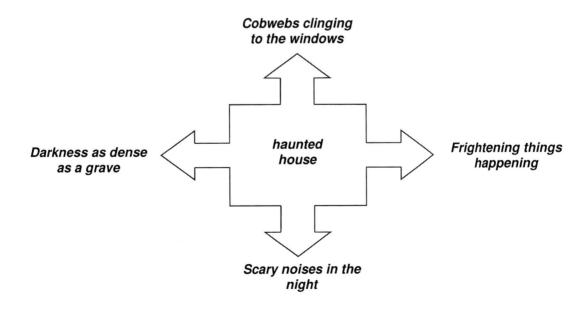

Similes -   ... as a ... sentences

Similes can be added as a further way of developing the initial brainstorm. As these can be over-used by pupils it is best to set a 'ceiling' on the number of similes to be used, as follows:

Teacher: I'd like to see no more than three similes in this story. Jot down any other ideas you have and keep them to use in another ghost story.

Younger children might find the concept of a simile difficult to grasp. If this occurs, call the simile an

... as a ... sentence

and model examples e.g.

The old man's face was as wrinkly and as dry <u>as a</u> wizened prune.

The scream was as high <u>as an</u> opera singer's top note.

The darkness in the house was as dense <u>as a</u> grave.

Pupils can then turn phrases, already written on the brainstorm poster, into similes.

e.g.

The cobwebs clinging to the windows glowed, even though the darkness was as dense as a grave.

O.I. sentences (Outside/inside) - how a character appears on the outside but really feels on the inside!

Prompt symbol used: ◀ ▶

O.I. sentences are made up of two related sentences. The second sentence, in brackets, contrasts the internal, true emotion with the false impression, given in the first sentence.

An example:

He smiled and shook the man's hand warmly. (Inside, however, he was more frightened than ever.)

O.I. sentences provide insights into a character's personality whilst encouraging pupils to use punctuation beyond full stop and capital letter. They also provide an excellent opportunity for the inclusion of an authorial intrusion (writer speaks to reader) and, as such, achieve part of Level 5 criteria (UK) *"Disruption of plot for effect".*

Multi-sensory locational writing and visualisation techniques

Prompt symbols used:

A multi-sensory approach helps to develop effective locational writing. Many pupils use only the sense of sight to describe a place. If pupils are encouraged to also describe what can be heard, felt, smelled or tasted (where appropriate) this really can help the reader to 'experience the setting'.

For example:

PLOT SKELETON 1

A house has a reputation for being haunted – strange things happen there.

Teacher: The plot skeleton mentions a house, but we know nothing about this house. Close your eyes and see if you can see it in your head. What does it look like? What can you hear? What is unusual about it? What makes you scared?

When cutting off the sense of sight, we stimulate pupils' imaginative thinking. Encouraging pupils to close their eyes and 'see in their heads' can produce effective and surprising results. The use of the question: "Is there anything unusual about it?" also assists in avoiding a bland description of a place, object, or person.

Atmosphere and 'mood'

Prompt symbols used:

Description of the weather can be used to create atmosphere/mood in a story. Pupils can be taught that by linking:

1.   the emotional state of the character,
2.   a description of the location,
3.   the weather,

'atmosphere' in the story can be conveyed.
The emotion symbols are included so that pupils make a visual link between the weather and a character's mood. The device of linking weather and mood is used to great effect by many writers.

If the weather is lovely, then a character's mood reflects this. When the clouds gather and a storm threatens, a more tense atmosphere is created and a character's emotions may follow suit.
This authorial device could be used to great effect in Plot Skeleton 2 -The Disappearing Hitch-hiker:

1. A person is driving to an old friend's in a town some miles away. The weather is lovely and

he/she is enjoying the drive.

When the emoticon symbol ☺ and the weather symbol ☁ are shown together, the pupil is encouraged to link description of good weather and happiness.

Later in the plot skeleton the following is included:

2. He/she loses track of time and doesn't realise it is getting late. It becomes dark and the weather gets worse. ☹ ☁   👁   👂

In this instance the weather symbol is shown together with an unhappy face, encouraging children to make the link between them.

Speech by and between characters ending with an exclamation mark

Prompts symbols used: " 🗣 !" " 🗣 !"

 We have provided prompts, on each skeleton, which remind children to include speech and other linked punctuation.

One piece of punctuation which children use infrequently is the 'echo exclamation mark'. This is used when a character repeats something another character has said, often in a shocked manner. e.g.

"We'll be able to leave in about six hours," he said.

"Six hours!" Kim yelled.

Teachers may wish to introduce 'echo exclamations' when expanding the plot skeletons.

STORIES TO SHARE

Exciting, published examples of ghost stories should be read in conjunction with the plot skeletons. Links between reading and the pupils' own writing can thereby be made explicit.

To this end, the following list links some of our plot skeletons to stories written by established authors. It must be stressed that children should not COPY the stories as read to them, but rather begin to see that, by changing the details of the story, plot structures can also be changed and adapted to produce a range of effective ghost stories. In Appendix 1 (page 71), Year six teacher Nicola Floyd explains that while her pupils found the plot skeletons useful, some preferred to introduce their own shock endings!

It might be helpful to tell children;

A PLOT SKELETON + YOUR IDEAS = A GOOD STORY

SUGGESTED READING LINKS

PLOT SKELETON 1: Lovers Parted By Death

The Man Who Didn't Believe In Ghosts, Sorche Nic Leodhas

PLOT SKELETON 2: The Disappearing Hitchhiker

Huw, Geoffrey Palmer and Noel Lloyd

PLOT SKELETON 3: A Ghostly Helping Hand

The Ghostly Earl, R Chetwynd-Hayes

PLOT SKELETON 4: We've Been Here Before

Through The Veil, Sir Arthur Conan Doyle

PLOT SKELETON 5: Get Out Of Our House!

The Ghosts Of Motley Hall, Richard Carpenter

PLOT SKELETON 7: Finding A Way Home

Up The Pier, Helen Cresswell

PLOT SKELETON 8: The Phantom Coach

The Phantom Coach, Amelia B Edwards

PLOT SKELETON 9: Back For Good

Hans And His Master, Ruth Manning-Sanders

PLOT SKELETON 10: A Promise From Beyond The Grave

John Charrington's Wedding, E Nesbit

PLOT SKELETON 11: An Ancient Object Calls Up A Ghost

Oh, Whistle And I'll Come To You My Lad, M.R. James ***WARNING: This is a very scary story!***

PLOT SKELETON 19: A Christmas Ghost Story

I'll Be Seeing You, Jill Bennett

PLOT SKELETON 21: Now You See Me, Now You Don't

Crossing Over, Catherine Storr

Not At Home, Jean Richardson

PLOT SKELETON 23 (Romans Remain)

A Legion Marching, John Hyman

PLOT SKELETON 24 (What a Trick)

Yesterday's Witch, Gahan Wilson

PLOT SKELETON 25 (Animal Instincts)

The Little Yellow Dog, Mary Williams

The Shepherd's Dog, Joyce Marsh

MAKING THE MOST OF PLOT SKELETONS

When David Wray and Maureen Lewis wrote their book: **Writing Frames: Scaffolding Children's Non-Fiction Writing in a Range of Genres** *(1997) (Reading and Language Information Centre, University of Reading)* it was clear that they did NOT intend to produce a series of photocopiable worksheets.

Unfortunately this is how many teachers have used their work.

Please don't do this with our plot skeletons! If they are photocopied and handed out without the necessary modelling and class/group discussion (as noted previously) their impact will, at best, be limited and, at worst, function as a mere time filler which could compound pupils' dislike of writing.

They **should** act as an aid to the developing self-confidence of pupils as independent writers. They do **NOT** constitute the only way to write ghost stories. Indeed, the best writers often break all the rules of a genre. The operative word, however, in the previous sentence, is 'rules'. It is the authors' contention that it is impossible to break rules if rules are not made explicit in the first place!

So, how do plot skeletons fit this construct?

We hope that they help to highlight the plot structures of many of the most common ghost stories. Once structural plot development has been made clear, pupils will more readily 'break the rules' and begin to write stories of greater structural complexity.

To reduce this argument to its simplest form: plot skeletons can be used in the classroom as a way of 'structuring for independence'. When using plot skeletons, we are scaffolding as an aid to independent writing rather than creating a straitjacket which inhibits creativity and reduces story writing to a mere set of formulas. Plot skeletons are tools to be used in a whole-school, 'staged-and-paced' approach to writing. The end result of this process is, hopefully, a school where:

The majority of pupils find writing non-threatening.
They enjoy it!
They are willing to break the rules.

Plot skeletons are not <u>the</u> answer, but they are a useful component in the teacher's 'kitbag' of writing ideas. A successful and sensible teacher will 'pick and mix' from a broad range of ideas drawn from the widest range of sources.

We hope that 'Ghost Story Plot Skeletons' will be a useful addition to your repertoire.

Alan Peat & Julie Barnfather

ASSESSING PUPILS' UNDERSTANDING OF A GENRE

Before you use the Plot Skeletons with a class of children, it would be useful to find out what they already know about ghost stories. The following activity provides a useful starting point which informs future teaching thereby addressing the needs of specific pupils.

To begin the assessment, pupils are given a copy of the sheet illustrated below.

GHOST STORY POSTER

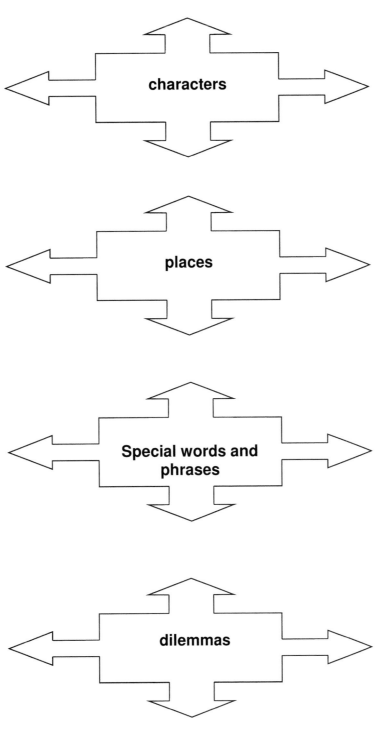

The pupils are then asked to complete the sheet in pairs. The teacher may wish to model how to achieve this by explaining that they want each pair to list as many characters as possible. With some groups it may be advisable to 'start them off' with an example:

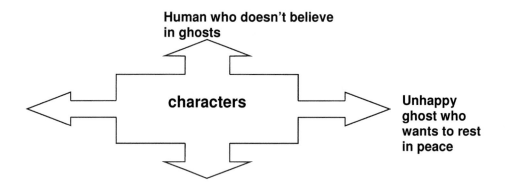

This process is repeated for **places** (e.g. haunted mansion), **special words and phrases** (e.g. moonlit winter's night) and **dilemma** (e.g. child is possessed).

With some groups of pupils, it may be useful to set numeric targets – *I wonder if you can beat ten ghost story characters.*

After about 15-20 mins. the teacher analyses the results and identifies areas for development. If, for example, the pupils have been able to name a significant number of characters BUT only two or three ghost story dilemmas, then 'dilemma' would, sensibly, form the focus of future teaching, thereby directly relating teaching to pupil learning needs.

If this approach is used in conjunction with plot skeletons, then the teacher is tackling both plot structure AND compositional elements of the form. This will help to develop a more rounded understanding of the particular genre. As a direct result of this, pupils will develop the self-confidence needed to take risks with both form and content.

This activity can easily be adapted to other narrative genres such as fairy tales, myths and legends etc. It provides the teacher with a very useful indicator of pupils' knowledge.

PLOT SKELETON 1

Lovers Parted By Death

1. A house has a reputation for being haunted – strange things happen there. 👁 👂 2A

2. The present owner was left the house by a distant relative, a farmer, who died at a very old age. 🗒

3. The farmer had one child, a beautiful daughter, who died as a teenager. ❗

4. The story the house owner has been told is that the farmer's daughter had been in love with a young man and he with her. They wanted to marry but his rich father had refused, so they met in secret. ◀ ▶

5. The owner has his own home so he rents out the house he has been left.

6. Several families try to live in the house but they are forced to leave by strange happenings. Everyone can hear strange things. Only children can see them. 👁 👂 "😨?" "🗣!"

7. The owner decides to move in and investigate.

8. When strange things happen, he ignores them. 👂

9. One day he goes into the attic. He finds a wardrobe full of the old farmer's clothes. [1] 📖

10. He also finds a wooden chest which belonged to the farmer's daughter. At the bottom of the chest, amongst more clothes, he finds a diary. [1] 📖 2A

11. He reads the diary which was written by the farmer's daughter. On the very last page he reads that she knew she was very ill and was going to die. Her final wish was to be buried beside her lover, wherever he is buried. [1] ☹

12. The owner does some research and finds that they were buried apart. He manages to change this. [1]

13. He decides to stay in the house and nothing strange ever happens again. ☺

PLOT SKELETON 2
The Disappearing Hitchhiker

1. A person is driving to see an old friend in a town some miles away. The weather is lovely and he/she is enjoying the drive. ☺ 🌥 👁 👂 👃

2. He/she loses track of time and doesn't realise it is getting late. It becomes dark and the weather worsens. ☹ 🌥 👁 👂

3. He/she almost runs out of petrol, but manages to find a garage just in time and sets off once again.

4. He/she suddenly spots a tall teenager, wearing a baseball cap, standing alone at the side of the road. 2A

5. The driver stops to offer a lift. The tall teenager silently gets into the car. "🗣 ?"

6. The driver tells the tall teenager he/she is going to his/her friend's in the town. The tall teenager tells the driver not to go to the town. "👤!"

7. They drive on in silence. When the driver looks around there is no one in the passenger seat.

8. The shocked driver stops in the next village and tells some people what has happened.

   "👤!" ❗

9. An old man asks what the teenager said. The driver explains and the old man tells him/her not

   to go to the town. "👤?"   "👤!"

10. The driver ignores the old man and sets off again. The weather is even worse. He/she no-

    tices a person waving by the roadside and stops to ask if they need help. "👤 ?"

11. The person walks to the car door and looks in. It is the same tall teenager the driver gave a

    lift to earlier. The teenager says: "Don't go to the town!" and then vanishes.   "👤!"

12. The driver is so frightened that he/she decides to spend the night at the next small hotel along

    the road. ☹

13. The hotel owner notices the driver is shaking and asks what is wrong. The driver tells him

    what had happened. The owner looks scared and tells the driver something terrible which

    happened many years before, to a tall teenager who always wore a baseball cap. ☹"👤!"

14. The next morning the driver sets off towards his/her friend's house.

15. Just outside the house, the driver stops. Something terrible has happened to the house dur-

    ing the night. The driver believes he/she would have died if he/she had not stayed at the hotel.

A REAL WARNING!

This is a story!
Don't forget that in real life you should NEVER get into a stranger's car.

PLOT SKELETON 3
A Ghostly Helping Hand

1. A ghost from the Victorian times haunts a well-know castle or mansion. It plays tricks on people and even though they are never hurt, they are always scared. The ghost has never been seen. ⊡ 👂 ☹

2. A family inherits the castle/mansion and moves in. $2A$

3. After a while, the son/daughter sees the ghost, is not scared and talks to it. "👤≼ !" ❗

4. The ghost tells the child its story. In life, it had been murdered by a person who also tried to cheat it and it can't rest peacefully. "🗣." 🖺

5. The child tells the rest of the family, but they don't believe him/her. "🗣!"

6. A few weeks later, the ghost overhears the parents telling the child that they can't afford to keep the castle/mansion, and may need to sell it. "🗣!" ☹

7. The ghost likes the child and decides to help. It remembers a story that, even before it had lived, treasure had been hidden somewhere in the castle. It decides to use its supernatural powers to find the treasure. ☐1

8. Some time later, a man arrives to discuss buying the castle/mansion. The ghost thinks it recognises him. "🗣?" ❗

9. The ghost watches and listens as the man tells them that his family had always wanted to live there. He tells them his name and the ghost suddenly knows that he is an ancestor of the person who had murdered and tried to cheat it! "🗣!"

10. The ghost does all sorts of horrible things to the man, who runs terrified from the house.

11. The family is still left with the problem of not being able to afford the castle/mansion.

12. The ghost searches everywhere and calls on its long-dead ancestors to help in the search. The ghost allows the child to help in the hunt. "🗣?" "🗣!"

13. They find a secret room which contains, among other things, a chest full of treasure. The child convinces his/her parents to come and look, and tells then about the ghost. "🗣." "🗣!" "🗣?"

14. The treasure is worth so much that the family is able to keep the castle/mansion. The child tells the ghost that they all want it to stay. "🗣!" ☺

PLOT SKELETON 4

"We've Been Here Before"

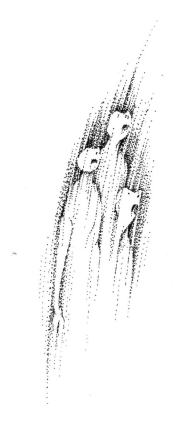

1. A young couple visits an ancient/very old site of interest (Roman Fort, Victorian house etc). 1 2A

2. They take a guided tour. The woman thinks she recognises the place, even though she knows she has never been there before. Both the man and the woman start to feel very sad.

3. Another person on the tour asks the guide a question about life in the past. The woman answers but doesn't know how she knows the answer. "🗣?" "🗣." 1

4. The guide continues to show people around. He/she tells a story about a sad thing that happened there long ago. The husband suddenly tells the guide he/she is wrong and explains what 'really' happened. "🗣!"

5. The guide disagrees and there is an argument. The puzzled man does not know how or why he knows the story. "🗣?" "🗣!" ◀ ▶

6. They continue to look around on their own and again find things they recognise or 'remember'.

7. It starts to get dark and the weather worsens. They leave the group to take shelter in an old building which they had not noticed before. After a while, they fall into a strange sleep.

8. The man dreams about the sad thing he had explained to the guide. It seems as if he is really there and the dream is real. The woman dreams the same thing and it also seems real to her.

9. The dream gets more and more frightening until one of them manages to do something in their dream which changes the sad end of the story they had told the guide into a happy ending.

10. When they wake up, they find they have slept all night and it is a beautiful sunny day. They leave their shelter and walk out into the site. The atmosphere feels happier.

11. The woman realises she has lost something. They return to where the old building was, but it is no longer there.

PLOT SKELETON 5
What A House Party!

1. In Victorian times, a group of rich people meets to spend a weekend at a
   country mansion which has a huge
   park around it. 1 👁 👂

2. There are three men and two women in
   the group. They all brought their own
   butlers and maids to look after them. 1

3. On the first evening together, they ask the host about the history of the house; when it was
   built, who used to live here etc. 1 "😫." "😫?" "😫!"

4. One lady jokingly asks if there is a ghost in the house. The host tells her that there is, and that
   the bedroom where she is sleeping is supposed to be haunted. "😫?" "😫!" ◀ ▶

5. The lady looks worried and the host tells her there is a bell-pull on the wall opposite her bed.
   When she pulls it, it will ring in her maid's room at the end of the corridor. She just has to get
   out of bed to ring that bell. ☹ "😫."

6. The friends enjoy a delicious meal and conversation. At about 11 o'clock, they go up to their
   rooms. 1

7. Early the next morning, the men meet to go for a walk around the estate. The ladies are still in their rooms.  👁

8. When the men return, the lady who slept in the haunted room is in the hall, ready to leave.

9. She tells the men she has had a terrible night. She went to sleep as usual, but woke in the middle of the night to see something very frightening in her room.

"😫?" "😫!" ❗ 2A

10. She was so shocked, she believes she fainted. When she woke up again, it was morning.

"😫!"

11. The lady's maid had told her she had heard the bell ring in the middle of the night. She rushed along the corridor into the lady's room. She saw nothing unusual, only her mistress, fast asleep. "😫."

12. The lady's carriage arrives and she and her maid drive off. 1

13. The shocked men look at each other in silence. Then one asks the question:
"If she fainted, she can't have moved out of her bed. So who rang the servant's bell?"

"😫?" "😫!"

PLOT SKELETON 6
"Get Out Of Our House!"

1. An old Victorian hall is up for sale. 1 👁 👂 2A

2. No one knows, but it has a 'staff' of ghosts including a butler and other servants. 1 👂

3. The ghosts can't leave the hall. ☹

4. It is important to them that they like the new owners. If they have to share 'their' hall, they feel they should have a say in who moves in! "😲!"

5. A series of people visit the hall to see if they want to buy it. First a family come, but the ghosts frighten them off. Next a head teacher comes and the ghosts frighten him/her off in a different way. 👁 👂 ☹ "🗣!" "😲!"

31

6. Finally a young couple visits the hall. The ghosts try to scare them but they are not afraid of anything the ghosts do. Eventually they make friends with the ghosts.

7. The couple buy the hall. The ghosts take on their old jobs and help the couple to live happily in their new home. ⬚1 ☺   ▤

PLOT SKELETON 7
Finding A Way Home

1. A young boy/girl has been sent away from home to stay with relatives at the seaside. He/she has been in trouble at school and his/her parents want him/her to stay away from a 'bad' group of young people.

    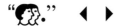

2. He/she is very angry, won't speak to anyone, won't talk to his/her parents on the phone and is determined not to enjoy the stay at the seaside.

3. One day he/she walks down to the seafront. He/she has been told it is exciting, but there is nothing there. No amusements, no fairground, only a pier with old kiosks.

4. He/she walks along the pier and sees a boy and girl playing. They are dressed in old fashioned clothes. 1

5. On the second day he/she walks along the pier once again and talks to the boy and girl.

6. On the third day they all begin to play together. The boy and girl have very strange toys and games. ⬜1

7. That night, he/she walks along the pier once again and sees the boy and girl are sleeping in one of the old kiosks on the pier. He/she asks why. "👥?"

8. They tell him their story. They have been evacuated from a big town nearby but the people they were due to stay with did not arrive to collect them from the train. They had no way of contacting their mum. "👥!"

9. The boy/girl realises the children are talking as if The Second World War is still happening! ⬜1

10. He/She tells them he/she will try to help. They tell him/her their address. "👥."

11. Back at the relative's house, he/she asks questions about the War then goes onto the Internet to do some research. ⬜1 "👥?"

12. He/she finds out that the address he/she had been given had been bombed the same day that the children were evacuated. Their mother had been killed. The boy/girl feels very sad. ☹ ❗

13. Worse still, the train on which the children had been travelling to the seaside had also been bombed. Two children had died on the train. ⬜1 🗐

14. The next day he/she returns to the pier. It has completely changed. It is now full of amusements, candy floss stands etc. 👁 👂 👃

15. At the end of the pier there are three figures waving goodbye. Two children – and a smiling lady. ☺ ☁

16. The girl/boy realises how lucky he/she is and looks forward to seeing his/her parents. ☺ ◀ ▶

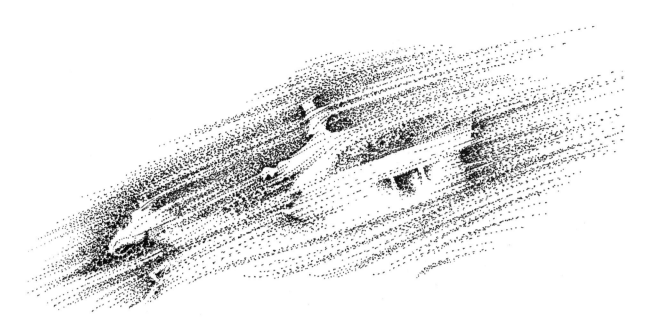

PLOT SKELETON 8
The Phantom Coach

1. I am going to tell you a story. I know it is true. It happened 20 years ago, in 1887. I have never told anyone this before. "🗣<." 1

2. I was out walking when I became lost. It began to snow. ☁ ☹

3. I knew I could not last the night out in the open and made my way towards a light. It was a house. I was given food, drink and shelter. 2A 👁 👃

4. The owner of the house was very strange. He told me a story about something that had happened that very night, three years earlier. ❗ "🗣."

5. He told me the mail coach had been travelling in a snow storm, the horses had slipped and the mail coach had toppled over a cliff. The two drivers and four men inside had died.

"🗣!" 1 📄

6. The weather seemed a little better so I decided to set off again. The owner of the house told me I would meet tonight's mail coach if I set off now and walked past the cliff on to the cross roads. It would take me about an hour, but the mail coach would stop there and I could get a ride.

7. I set off. I was frightened and felt strange.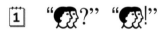

8. I lost track of time as it became darker and was surprised when I heard the mail coach coming up behind me. It stopped and its two drivers nodded when I asked if I they would give me a lift. " 🗣< ?" ❗

9. I climbed inside and although it was dark, I could see there were three men inside the coach.

10. I tried to make conversation, but none of the men would talk. " 🗣< ."

11. I realised something was wrong with the coach and the men inside. I tried to get out but couldn't. ◀ ▶

12. I then heard screaming, felt as if I was flying through the air and then passed out.

13. I woke up in bed at home two days later. I had been found in a snowdrift exactly where the coach had crashed three years ago.

    1️⃣   "🗣?" "🗣!"

14. Nothing else was found there.

PLOT SKELETON 9
Back For Good

1. A selfish, rich old man died and was buried in the family vault.
   He left all of his money to his widow, making her very rich indeed. [1] ❢

2. They had no children and the man had fallen out with his only brother years ago.

3. After his funeral, his widow and all the servants in the mansion were disturbed by strange things happening in the house, especially at night.

4. This went on for weeks and the widow was upset, scared and puzzled. ☹

5. Unexpectedly, the dead man's brother arrived. He had been abroad for a long time and had only just heard of his brother's death. "." ☹   2A

6. The widow invited him to stay at the mansion for as long as he wanted. "?" "."

7. For the first three nights, for the first time since the funeral, the house was peaceful. The servants slept. The widow slept. 😐

8. The dead man's brother also slept, but he always dreamt that his brother was trying to tell him something. "!"

9. He told the widow about his dream and they decided to sit up together to see if the dead man would try to contact them. "😲!"

10. At some point in the night, something strange happened to a piece of furniture in the room.

2A 👁 👂

11. Inside/under/upon that piece of furniture, a new copy of the dead man's will appeared. In it he left a third of his money to his brother (along with a message), a third to charity and a third to his widow. "🗣." 1 😐

12. The widow was happy to share the fortune. Once this was done, the strange things stopped happening. "😲?" "😲!" ☺

PLOT SKELETON 10
A Promise From Beyond The Grave

1. A young couple love each other very much and decide to get married. ! 2A

2. The date is set and preparations are made. ☺

3. Two days before the wedding, the groom has to travel away to visit an elderly relative. "●."

4. His bride-to-be begs him not to go, saying she has dreamt that he won't return. "●!"

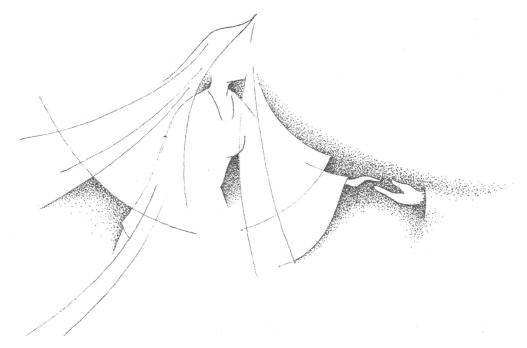

5. The grooms "swears on his life" that <u>nothing</u> will stop him from being at their wedding. They say goodbye and he leaves. "●!" ☹

6. The day of the wedding arrives but the groom has not returned. ☹

7. An hour before the ceremony is due to take place, the Best Man receives an urgent message from the groom to meet him at his house.

8. The best man rushes to the house, but the groom is not there. Half an hour before the wedding, the Best Man leaves for the church without the groom.

9. When he gets to the church, the doors are closed and the wedding is taking place.

10. A bystander tells him the groom arrived by taxi at the very last minute.

11. Another person tells the best man the groom's appearance was very strange.

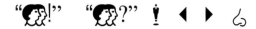

12. At length, the bride and groom come out of the church, get straight into a waiting taxi and drive off at speed. ❗

13. Everyone gets into their cars and follows the taxi. Suddenly the taxi screeches to a halt at the side of the road.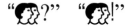

14 The bride's father opens the back door of the taxi. His daughter has fainted and the groom has vanished. ❗

15. At that very moment a phone call comes through on the Best Man's mobile phone. He answers and a policeman tells him he has bad news. The groom was killed three hours ago in a car accident. The Best Man's number was the last number dialled on the phone.

"🗯?" "🗯!"

16. The bride never recovered.

PLOT SKELETON 11
An Ancient Object Calls Up A Ghost

1. A man/woman sets off to spend some time alone on holiday in a very peaceful, remote place.

2. He/she meets a doctor on several occasions. They chat about everyday things such as the weather, the holiday resort etc.

3. A few days later, the man/woman finds something, an ancient object, such as a toy, a musical instrument (or any object which can be used to <u>do</u> something.)

4. After the object is found, and used, a number of strange things happen to the man/woman.

5. He/she tries to make the scary things stop but can't stop them. He/she becomes very worried and nervous.

6. The doctor notices the effect the frightening things have had on his/her companion, listens to the story, and offers to help.

7. Together they face the ghost, which has become even worse than before. They try to make it go away.

8. Nothing seems to be working. The doctor asks when the frightening things started to happen and the man/woman remembers that it was after he/she had found, and used the object.

"?" "!" ⅰ 2A

9. Together they destroy the object and the frightening things stop forever. ☁ ☺

PLOT
SKELETON 12
It's MY House!

1. A middle aged couple sells a business and house in town to buy and move into a beautiful house in the country. The old man who lived there has died and the couple have bought the house from his solicitors.

2. Their first summer is lovely. They love the house and their life in the country.

👁 👂 2A ☁☺

3. In September an air mail letter arrives from a man who claims the house they have bought belongs to HIM. He is very rude and insulting to the couple. "😠?" "😠!"

4. He claims the old man was his uncle, and the house they are living in had been left to HIM in the old man's will. He lives far away and is flying over to sort out the matter. The couple knows there is going to be trouble. "🗣!"

43

5. They talk to the solicitor who tells them the old man HAD made a will, but one day came to see him, tore up the will in front of him and left. The old man died a few weeks later.

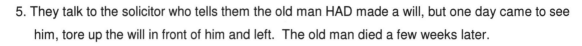

6. The couple is dreading the man's arrival. Then they get the news that his plane has crashed. The man is listed among the dead.

7. That night, strange things begin to happen in the house. It seems as if a 'presence' is looking for something but can't find it. 👁 〗 ☁ ☹

8. This continues for months. The couple begin to see the 'ghost'. It starts to appear more and more often. Their life becomes miserable. ☹   👁

9. Finally the middle aged man living in the house decides to tell the ghost to leave. ◀ ▶

10. The ghost does many more frightening things because it is angry. Suddenly the middle aged man falls to the ground. He is dead. "🗣!"

11. His widow leaves the house and never returns. ☁ ☹

12. The house is now up for rent. A couple is walking toward it with the front door keys …
"🗣."

PLOT SKELETON 13
A Ghostly Love Story

1. A widow, on holiday, drives past a house she really likes. She sees it is up for rent.

2. She contacts the estate agent to make an appointment to see inside.

3. She finds it hasn't been lived in for a long time and asks why. The estate agent says he does-n't know, but the woman feels that he is lying.

4. She loves the house and moves in. In a short time she is happier than she has been for a long time.

5. Strange things start to happen and the widow begins to feel that something is trying to make her leave the house. 😐

6. She is determined to stay, so when the strange things happen, she talks to the ghost, telling it she isn't frightened. "😕?" "😕!"

7. Whatever the ghost does, she refuses to be scared.

8. The 'strange' things stop being annoying. Things began to happen which help the widow.

9. She starts to talk to whatever is helping her. "😕."

10. One day she asks the ghost to show itself. The figure of a man appears. "😕?"

11. He begins to visit the widow every day and they enjoy talking together. "😕."

12. After a while the widow's daughter visits and tells her mum that she needs to get out and about more and possibly meet someone else. "😕!"

13. The widow says that she doesn't need to. The ghost overhears.

15. The next day the widow talks to the ghost. There is no reply and the ghost never appears again. "🗣 ?"

16. The widow misses the ghost but stays in the house. 😐

17. Twenty years later, the widow dies, in her bedroom in the house.

18. At the bottom of the bed, the ghost appears. He has been waiting for her …

46

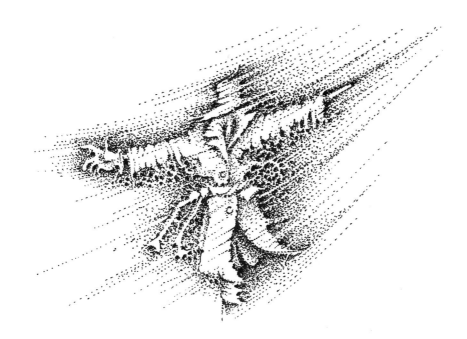

PLOT SKELETON 14
The Scarecrow

1. A family goes on holiday in the countryside in a beautiful rented cottage. 👁 👂

2. In the farmer's field next to the cottage there is a scarecrow. The whole family thinks it looks

   evil. 2A "😱!"

3. The oldest child has to sleep downstairs in the living room because his/her mum and dad want

   the master bedroom and his/her brother wants the other bedroom. ☹

4. The next morning the family goes out but for some reason, the oldest child stays in the cottage.

   ☹   "😱!" "😱?"

5. He/she is in the kitchen when the phone rings.   👂

6. He/she answers it but the only sound to be heard is breathing. They hang up. 👂

47

7. He/she starts to feel scared, as if someone is watching them. ☹

8. Back in the kitchen, he/she looks out of the window. The scarecrow has gone. 👁

9. He/she is getting more scared. He/she turns on the TV but it doesn't work properly.

     ☹   👁   👂

10. There is knock on the door. 👂

11. He/she looks out of the window by the door. There is no one there. ☹

12. He/she tries to ring his/her mum's mobile. It rings in his/her parent's bedroom so he/she runs
    into the bedroom.

13. The scarecrow is standing 'looking through' the window. 👁   2A

15. The child is terrified. ☹   ☹   ☹

16. His/her mum's mobile phone rings again.

17. He/she answers it. "🗣 !"   "🗣 ?"

18. All he/she can hear is hysterical laughing. "🗣 !"   "🗣 ?"

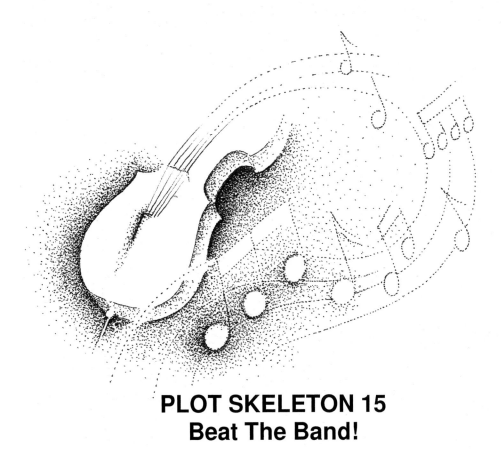

PLOT SKELETON 15
Beat The Band!

1. After leaving university, a group of friends rents a large house together in order to save money.

   It is actually an old school which has been renovated.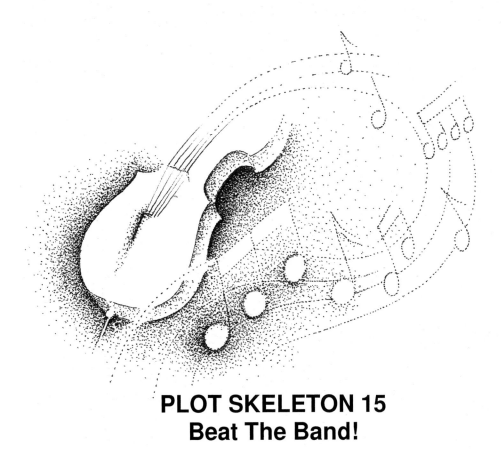

2. Almost immediately things strange things begin to happen. At different times of the day, loud

   music can be heard in the whole building. Everyone hears it.

3. The people in the house blame this on young children in the neighbourhood. 2A

4. The music starts to annoy all of them. Finally they contact the owner of the building. He says he

   has never heard music before but the friends don't believe him.

5. They are sure a rock band has found a secret way into the basement to practice there.

6. They decide to catch the culprits and put an end to the noise.

7. They invite some other friends to join them one evening.

8. The music starts again and they all hunt through the big, old building. They all carry torches.

9. They follow the sound down into the basement, where they find an old wall which has been boarded up.

10. The sound is so loud that the floorboards in front of the boarded up wall are vibrating.

11. They knock down the wooden wall and shine their torches into an old, dusty, totally empty hall. There is complete silence. 👁

12. The friends who joined in the search laugh and cheer. They think it is a clever trick but the people who live there stand silently. Not one of them laughs. "😕?" "😕!"

PLOT SKELETON 16
A Pet Farewell

1. A family's cat dies very suddenly. He had been young and in good health, so the family never

    had the chance to say goodbye. ☹   *2A*

2. Almost a year passes by and the family is aware that January 16th, the day of their pet's death,

    is fast approaching.

3. The youngest child in the family is very upset when he remembers his/her pet. "🗯."

4. On January 16th the family waits until the exact time their cat had died, then gathers together at

    his grave in the garden. "🗯."

5. Suddenly they hear a meow. Everyone jumps and looks round. They all see their cat, running above the snow in the garden.

6. No-one can believe it, the whole family is shocked. "🤯?" "🤯!"

7. The youngest child runs forwards and strokes the purring cat. It is warm and as affectionate as it had been in the past.

☺ 2A

8. The cat then goes to each member of the family, giving them a chance to hold and stroke it.

☺

9. After a few minutes the cat seems to decide he has stayed long enough.

10. Watched by the whole family, the cat runs to the bottom of the garden, then slowly fades away. ☹   😐

PLOT SKELETON 17
The Lost Gift

1. A nurse working at a small hospital goes in to work as usual at the start of her shift.

2. She is wearing a pair of small gold earrings that she loves. Her father had given them to her, just before he died, a year ago. 😐

3. She and the other nurse on duty that day share out the rooms in which they care for the patients. The nurse wearing earrings is given rooms 111 – 120 while the other nurse will work in rooms 104 – 110. "👥?" "👥."

4. In room 120, our nurse helps a patient who is very ill. She has to wear a tight face mask every time she goes in to the room, to prevent germs. 👁   👂

5. At lunchtime the nurse realizes she is wearing only one earring. The other is missing. She searches every room she has worked in but she can't find it. ☹

6. She thinks that she might have lost it as she took off the face mask when she was leaving room 120. She checks room 120 really carefully, but finds nothing.

7. She tells all of the members of staff in the hospital what has happened, but no one has seen the earring. She goes home feeling very sad indeed.

8. The next day, the nurse receives a phone call from the housekeeper at the hospital. The earring has been found, in Room 110, under the mattress.

9. The nurse can't believe it. She didn't go near Room 110 yesterday, but not only that, Room 110 is the room in which her father had died exactly one year ago.

PLOT SKELETON 18
Foggy Life-Saver

1. A woman is driving her children home late at night. It is very foggy and she has trouble seeing very far ahead in the road. 👁 2A 🌫☹

2. She puts on the car radio to keep her children entertained on the journey. Soon they fall asleep. 👂

3. The fog worsens and the woman is working out the safest way home. "🗣 !"

4. She takes the dual carriageway and although she can barely see, she remembers it goes up a hill just before a turn off to her home.

5. The roads are virtually empty. The lady is in the right hand, faster lane of the dual carriageway as she approaches the bottom of the hill. She decides to move into the slower left-hand lane. "🗣."

6. As she moves across, she thinks she hears a voice say: "Get back in the fast lane". "😠!"

7. She ignores it, but a minute later, she hears it again, even louder than before. "😠!"

8. She does what she is told, moves into the fast lane and starts to go up the hill. ◀ ▶

9. Suddenly she realises she is passing a car which is stuck in the left hand lane. People are trying to push it out of the way. She misses hitting the back of the car by just millimetres.

10. As she starts to go safely down the other side of the hill, she realises the radio is still playing loudly. How has she heard anything at all? What did she hear?

55

PLOT SKELETON 19
A Christmas Ghost Story

1.   It is a family Christmas. In the house there are two teenage boys, their mum and their

step-father. 👁 👂 📖

2. On Christmas Eve they learn they are going to have an unexpected guest, a relative, for

Christmas. "🗣." "🗣!"

3. The boys realise they will have to share a bedroom and they aren't very happy. "🗣!"

4. The younger boy has bought presents for everyone and only has enough pocket money left to
buy himself something. He is now expected to buy something for the new visitor. He is even

more unhappy than he was before! "🗣 !"

5. He is sent to do some last minute shopping for his family and told to buy the final present from

his own money. "🗣!"

6. After wandering round the shops he stumbles into a second hand shop he has never seen
before. He finds something that looks very expensive, but isn't. He decides to buy it and still has

money left for himself. 👁 "🗣." 📧

7. The guest arrives. On Christmas Day he/she is given presents from the family. The younger
   boy's present surprises everyone because it looks so good and the new guest loves it. He/she
   looks at it/play with it/watches it all day. "🗣." "🗣!" "🗣?" ☺

8. Strange things then began to happen. Every time the new guest says something complimen-
   tary to a member of the family, something nasty happens to that family member. "🗣."

9. The youngest boy notices and begins to wonder if it has something to do with his present. He
   feels guilty about how mean he has been. 😕

10. Something rather nasty happens to each member of the family through the day. Each incident
    is worse than the last.   It isn't a great Christmas Day! 📧

11. Eventually everyone goes to bed. The new guest takes the "special" present up with him/her.

12. During the night something awful happens. It is much worse then anything that has happened
    throughout the day.

13. The family has to flee the home. 👁   👂   2A

14. Their guest goes home earlier than planned. As he/she gets into the car, the youngest boy
    gets the strangest feeling that somehow he/she knows how mean he has been with his last-
    minute present!

PLOT SKELETON 20
Cabin 502

1. A man books a trip on a boat.

2. He arrives on board and tells the purser his cabin number. The purser looks surprised but gives directions to the cabin. 👁 👂 "🗣?" "🗣."

3. In the cabin there are two bunks. The man chooses the bottom bunk, puts his/her bag on it then goes out to explore the boat.

4. After dinner, the man goes back to the cabin and turns in for the night.

5. In a little while, he sees the cabin door open. His room-mate comes in, climbs onto the top bunk and settles down to sleep. They say nothing to each other. 2A

6. In the middle of the night the man hears an awful scream and wakes up to see that the cabin door is wide open. The bunk above is empty. "🗣 !"

7. He calls a steward and the ship is searched for the missing room-mate but he has disappeared. "🗣!" "🗣?"

8. The man goes back to his/her cabin. The porthole is wide open. 👁

9. He closes it and gets back into bed to go to sleep. Three times in the night he wakes suddenly

   to find the porthole open. Each time he closes it and goes back to sleep. 👁

10. The next morning, the man is walking up on deck thinking about the strange happenings in his

    cabin. He bumps into the ship's captain, who tells him that two other passengers have disap-

    peared from his cabin on previous journeys. "🗣." "🗣!"

11. The captain offers to arrange a different cabin for the man but he refuses, determined to find

    out what is going on. "🗣?"

12. That night the man goes to his cabin to settle down for the night. He makes sure the porthole

    is bolted and locked and that the cabin door is also bolted and locked. He goes to sleep.

13. In the middle of the night, he wakes to find the porthole wide open. He gets up to close it, then

    realises:
    a. He can smell something.   👃

b. He can see something in the top bunk. 2A

14. He switches on the light. There is nothing there, but the bunk is soaking wet and the smell is

    awful.

15. He stays awake for the rest of the night. The next day, he asks the captain for his help in solv-

    ing the mystery. "🗣?"

16. They decide to sit up all night in the cabin. During the night, the locked porthole opens three

    times. On the last time, they actually watch as the screws turn - by themselves! ☹

17. After the third time, they call the ship's carpenter who nails the porthole shut.

18. The porthole opens again, right in front of their eyes. The lights in the cabin go out.

19. An awful smell comes from the top bunk and the terrified captain and passenger run from the

    cabin. The captain orders that the cabin should be locked and nailed closed. No other passen-

    gers ever stay in cabin 502.

PLOT SKELETON 21
Home Alone

1. A teenager is asked out on a Friday night by someone he/she really likes.

2. He/she rushes home to get ready and finds his/her mum getting ready to go out. There is a family emergency she must attend to and she asks the teenager to look after his/her younger brother/sister.

3. The teenager is very disappointed and angry. He/she argues and tells his/her mother about being asked out.

4. Mum is very sorry, but she must go and there is no-one else to look after the younger child. She leaves the house.

5. The teenager accepts there is nothing he/she can do. At bedtime, he/she reads a story to the younger child, who falls asleep quickly.

6. The child is sleeping soundly and the teenager decides there will be no harm in him/her slipping out to meet his/her date.

7. The teenager leaves the house, locks the doors and sets off for the arranged meeting place.

8. On the way, the teenager passes a friend in the street. He/she greets the friend, but they ignore him/her. "👤!" "👤?"

9. The teenager reaches the meeting place just a few minutes later than planned. The date is still there. The teenager rushes over and says hello. His/her date ignores the teenager completely, then turns his/her back and walks away. "👤!"

10. The upset teenager makes his/her way home. Closer to the house, the teenager hears sirens and starts to run, suddenly worried. ☹ 👂 👃

11. He/she sees his/her mother, weeping hysterically. Behind her are an ambulance and a fire engine. Behind them is his/her fire-damaged home. 👁 2A 👂

12. The teenager rushes, shouting, into the crowd, but people ignore him/her. "👤!"

13. He/she stops and hears a fireman explaining what has happened to his/her mum. Two bodies have been found in the small bedroom of the house. "👤." "👤?"

PLOT SKELETON 22
The Haunted House of Ancient Rome

1. It is the 2nd century A.D. A philosopher has just arrived in Rome and he needs to find a home.

2. The property agent shows the philosopher a beautiful house that he can rent very cheaply. 2A

3. The philosopher is suspicious and asks if there is something wrong with the house. "?"

4. The agent laughs nervously and says he is sure the house is fine, despite the rumours. He says he has never seen anything unusual. "!"

5. The philosopher asks about the rumours. The agent tells him that the house is said to be haunted by a hideous, angry old man whose thin legs and arms are weighed down with heavy shackles and chains. "?" "!"

6. The house was last rented to a group of young men who hired the house as a dare. All five left, terrified and within a year they were all dead. "."

7. The philosopher realises he can strike a bargain. He says he will take the house if the rent is halved. The agent agrees. "?" "."

8. The philosopher moves into the house two days later. He is working late and hears a terrible clanking and wailing. It becomes louder and louder. Something is moving towards the study.

9. The philosopher works on, ignoring the noise. ◀ ▶

10. When the ghost reaches the study, it sees the philosopher and decides he will be its new victim.

11. The ghost shakes its chains and moans fiercely. The philosopher continues working. The ghost moves closer, making an awful noise. $2A$

12. The philosopher tells the ghost to be quiet. Secretly he is frightened, but doesn't show his fear. "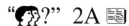!" ◀ ▶

13. The ghost stops and steps back. He starts to think the philosopher might be able to help. No one has EVER talked to it! He moans quietly. "🗣!"

14. The philosopher asks the ghost what it wants. "?"

15. The ghost beckons the philosopher with its finger and he follows it into the garden. The ghost points to the ground sadly, then disappears. $2A$ ☹

16. The philosopher marks the spot, then, exhausted, goes to bed.

17 The next morning, the philosopher goes to the magistrates and gets permission to investigate in the garden. After digging for some time, he finds a skeleton with chains on its arms and legs. Was it a slave killed by a cruel master, or a prisoner of some kind?

"?" $2A$ 📰

18. The philosopher arranges a proper burial for the skeleton, then sends for a priest to cleanse the house.

9. He is left alone in his beautiful, peaceful house. ☺

PLOT SKELETON 23
Romans Remain

1. Two friends are enjoying a summer day out in the countryside. They have just finished junior school and started their summer holiday. ☁ ☺ 👁 👂

2. They wander out of town, along the old Roman Road they have been learning about in history. 🗒1

3. On their walk, they talk about who and what might have travelled down that road in the past. 🗒1 "👥?" "👥." 2A

4. They are enjoying themselves so much that they don't realise how late it has become.

5. The sky grows darker and an unusual noise startles them. They realise it is time to return home. 👂 ☹☁

6. They are about to turn around, when they see a figure, dressed very unusually, walking to-wards them along the road. ❗ 📑

7. They crouch at the side of the road. The figure which has startled them silently passes by.

8. The friends run home, terrified. When they get back, they discuss what they have seen.

☹   "👥?" "👥!" ①

9. One of them decides to go back the next night and begs his/her friend to go along too.

"👥!"

10. The friend doesn't want to, but agrees to please his/her friend. They arrange to meet at a certain place on the Roman Road.

11. The next day, he/she changes his/her mind. He/she rings to tell his/her friend, but he/she has already left! "🗣 !"

12. The second friend has an awful feeling that his/her friend is in danger. He/she sets off to catch up. ☹

13. The first friend is a long way off in the distance and the second can't catch up. He/she shouts, but gets no reply.

14. The first friend reaches the point where the incident happened the day before. The second watches from a distance.

15. At exactly the same time as the night before, the same apparition walks along the road toward the friends. ❗

16. The second friend watches helplessly as he/she hears his/her friend loudly say something in Latin. ①

17. The second friend runs towards his/her friend. Suddenly, he/she trips and falls down. When he/she stands again, he/she can see his/her friend walking alongside the figure and disappearing over the brow of the hill. The friend is never seen again. The police ask questions and search, but he/she is never found. The second friend is now learning Latin ... 2A "🗣 !"

PLOT SKELETON 24
What a Trick!

1. A group of five friends is getting ready to go out 'trick-or-treating' early on Halloween evening.

2. Each of them is wearing a costume and they are all excited about tricking their neighbours and the treats they will be given. 2A

3. Their parents have told them not to go further than three streets from their homes. They must also return by 8.30. This is the first year that they have been allowed to go out without an adult.

4. They put the final touches to their costumes and set out.

5. The oldest boy's mum calls him back and tells him to look after the others. She reminds him that they MUST be back by 8.30pm.

6. They set out and have a great time. They collect lots of goodies.

7. By 8.00pm they have knocked on all of the houses in the three streets, but don't want to go home.

8. The oldest boy suggests they knock on the door of a really spooky, dark house just past the graveyard. They have never been there before and it is further away than the three streets.

9. The others agree – if he will go first! "😬!"

10. He makes his way down the path, and reaches up to ring the bell. Before his finger reaches the bell, the door swings open and an old lady stands in a brightly-lit, welcoming hallway. The boy can smell freshly baked cookies, cakes and fresh apples. 👁 2A 📑 ❗ ✍

11. The old lady tells the boy to bring his friends over and they all cluster into the hall and have their bags filled with treats.

12. Very soon all of the goodies have disappeared into their bags, so the children say goodbye to the old lady and set off home, chattering at the tops of their voices.

13. They pause at the gate to wave. The door is closed and the house is in darkness again. Somehow it looks even spookier than it did before. ☹ ☁

14. The children start to make their way home, thinking about the wonderful treats they have in their bags.

15. Suddenly the eldest boy stops in his tracks. He can hear him mum frantically calling his name. The others start to hear their parents' voices too. "🗣 !"

16. They start to run and bump into a search party of parents out hunting for them. ☹

17. The eldest boy asks his mum what is wrong and she starts to shout at him for not being back in time and for being out of the agreed area. "😬?" "😬!"

18. The oldest boy starts to argue, saying it can't be any later than 8.15, and shows his mum his watch. It has stopped at 8.07.

19. His mum points up at the church clock: it is five to midnight.

20. The children slowly follow their parents home. One by one they open their bags of sweets. Everything the old lady gave them has turned to ashes. ☹

PLOT SKELETON 25
ANIMAL INSTINCTS

1. A small dog is running along a beach on a, hot, sunny day.

2. It runs up to a boy/girl playing on the beach.

3. The boy/girl is very lonely and is glad to have someone to play with. He/she talks to the dog as if it can understand and asks it all kinds of questions.

4. They play in the sea and sand for a while, until the boy/girl's aunt shouts for him/her to come in for tea.

5. The boy/girl runs off. He/she is staying with an aunt in a house beside the beach. He/she is enjoying him/herself but has no friends to play with.

6. He/she pauses at the door of the cottage for a second to wave goodbye to the dog.

7. His/her aunt looks out of the window but she doesn't see anyone on the empty beach. 2A

8. The boy/girl wakes up very early the next day. The little dog is on the beach waiting. They play for a while, then the dog runs off.

9. The boy/girl runs home for dinner. His/her aunt asks what he/she had been doing. When the boy/girl tells her about the dog, she looks puzzled. She has been looking out of the window all morning but hasn't seen a dog. "🗣?" "🗣?"

10. That afternoon, a sad-looking old man wanders along the beach. He asks the boy/girl if he/she has seen a dog, and describes the dog the boy/girl has been playing with. ❗

    "🗣?"

11. The boy/girl tells the old man what has happened. He looks sad and walks away. 2A

12. The next day, exactly the same things happen (the dog is waiting, plays, then runs away). The old man appears and once more, asks about it. Something about the old man makes the boy/girl feel very sad. ☹

13. He/she is determined to find out what is wrong, so the next day, when the dog runs away, the boy/girl follows. The dog runs to an old cave at the bottom of a cliff and once inside, starts to dig. It looks at the boy/girl as if asking for help. 🗒 👁 👂 ✋

14. The boy/girl joins in, digging with his/her hands in the sand. Suddenly, the dog jumps out of the hole and runs away. The boy/girl keeps digging for a few minutes, then his/her fingers brush something hard. Under the sand is the skeleton of a dog. 👁 ☹

15. The boy/girl leaves the cave and walks back along the beach. In the same place as normal, the old man is standing patiently. He asks again about the dog. "🗣?" "🗣!"

16. The boy/girl tells him about the dog and the skeleton in the cave. The man smiles strangely then walks off in the direction of the cliffs. "🗣!"

17. That night, just before darkness falls, the boy/girl looks out of the cottage window. In the distance, he/she sees the same old man throwing a stick for a little dog. 👁 ☺

APPENDIX 1

PLOT SKELETONS IN THE CLASSROOM

Nicola Floyd, Year 6 teacher, Hazel Slade Primary School, Cannock, Staffordshire

We started by deconstructing an extract from *Tom's Midnight Garden* (the part where the Hall comes to life and the ghostly maid appears). As I read the story I paused at the end of each paragraph and asked a child to scribe on the whiteboard the class summary of what had happened. This way we built our own skeleton.

Once the children understood skeletal story outlines, I felt they needed to understand the icons used in your book. We discussed what each was and asked for examples to remind the children of the techniques. This was easy, as *Show Not Tell*, *O.I.* sentences etc. are part of the children's normal Literacy vocabulary.

The next stage, and a vital stage I felt, was working together to show how these story plots could come to life and this was where I introduced drama.
The first plot skeleton we used was 'A Foggy Life-Saver'. I divided the children into 6 groups and gave each one a section of the story that had some icons next to them. The children worked in these groups to tell their section of the story—including sound effects. Point three was really interesting as the children decided to sing Christmas carols for the music on the radio. We then put all the parts together in a whole class performance. I acted as a narrator and told parts of the story without icons next to them. The children really enjoyed this.

From this stage we needed to look at how this atmosphere could be recreated in writing. We took a new plot, *The Scarecrow*, and first of all decided on which parts of the story we wanted to add the most meat to! Many children chose the description of the scarecrow and the feeling of the child, so that is what we explored next. As a class we mapped out some ideas about what the scarecrow might be like and filled in the *Show Not Tell* grid for 'scared' to show how the main character was feeling. The children then chose whether to work alone or in pairs. Some children used small whiteboards first to try out ideas before committing themselves to paper— which I felt really helped the more reluctant writers.

The children have used a few of the skeletons and found them useful. The general feelings were that having the outline and knowing where the story was going allowed them to focus on the actual detail they were including. Some children liked having the icons to guide them to the tools they could include in that part of the story. A few children, though, felt a little restricted— particularly with having the ending organised for them, and so I suggested they could add a shock ending of their own!

APPENDIX 2
Example of story written using Plot Skeleton 14
The Scarecrow
By Daniella Spittle and Emily Morris
Year 6, Hazel Slade Primary School, Cannock, Staffordshire

Is it the cottage where the trees are swaying?
Is it the cottage with beautiful hanging baskets that make the birds sing?
Is the cottage where fields go on for miles, with sheep grazing in them?
Yes, but it is not all nice! Let me tell you all about it.

It all began one day when my family and I went on holiday to a rented cottage. There was a tall, hollow scarecrow standing sternly facing our cottage. We all thought it looked a little evil.

I had to sleep downstairs being as I was the eldest. Mum and Dad wanted the master bedroom and Sam (my younger brother) wanted the other room. I was a little annoyed that I had to sleep on the uncomfortable sofa, but then again, I was the oldest!

The next morning, Mum, Dad and Sam went out shopping. But I stayed at home because shopping is so boring. I was quite excited but I was also a little nervous. I kept on peering out of the window to check on that funny looking scarecrow. I was just about to make myself a cup of tea when the phone rang. I wondered whether to answer it. Mum had always told be not to answer the phone when I was alone. I ignored her advice and answered it. No one was there; all I could hear was heavy breathing. I decided to hang up.

I started to shiver as my knees trembled and knocked together. My mouth went dry. A sudden chill travelled down my spine. I thought someone was watching me. I began to wonder who was on the phone.

I went back to the kitchen, with my legs still trembling. I peered out the window and the scarecrow had gone. On the outside, I looked calm and brave but on the inside my heart was beating like a drum.

I started to shake madly. I thought to myself what could pass the time away. Automatically I thought of the T.V. but it didn't work. I knew it was linked to the scarecrow!

I heard a knock at the door. I darted to the door hoping that it would be Mum, Dad and Sam. I looked out of the window. No one was there; my heart began to beat faster.

I ran to the phone to ring Mum. I could hear her mobile phone ring up stairs, in my left ear. So I ran to the master bedroom. And as I opened the door and in front of me, outside the window, was the scarecrow.

The dark, black scarecrow was staring at me through the window. I nearly fainted in fear. I was absolutely terrified.

I heard my Mum's phone ring again. I grabbed it off her bedside table and answered it. I shrieked in shock. I was totally confused.

All I could hear was a cheeky laugh. I could definitely tell who it was. It was Sam. I was so embarrassed and a bit annoyed with him.

"Don't ever do that to me again, you evil boy!" I yelled.

APPENDIX 3
Illustrating the stories—Glyn Matthews

We asked Glyn to explain how he produced the illustrations for Ghost Story Plot Skeletons. If you look closely, you can see they are made up of thousands of tiny dots and if you want to, you can have a go too...

Glyn says: "It's not strenuous. You don't need running shoes—although it could end up a marathon!

You need a pen and paper, but this is Art not English. It's a drawing exercise but you don't need to be any good at drawing! You don't need a huge piece of paper and it would be best if your pen has black ink and a fine tip—good for making dots, the smaller the better. You will need some patience, so make sure you don't need the loo before you start. But, you don't need to concentrate—well, not too hard anyway.

Here's what you do -

Get yourself comfy—you can do this on your knee in front of the T.V. if you want, but make sure you rest your paper on something firm (not the cat). Actually, I sometimes use my cat as a rest (Boris is his name, he thinks he's a dog, but that's another story). Anyway, get your pen poised because you're going to start dotting. That's right, dotting. Imagine that your pen tip is a bird's beak and it's hungry (and pretty stupid because there's nothing really to peck at on the piece of paper), but start pecking anyway—think "crazy chicken" and you won't go far wrong.

"But what am I going to draw?" I hear you cry. That's just it—don't try to draw anything, you'll spoil it if you do. Just keep dotting, like lots of full stops. Be careful not to let them become commas—no tadpoles either, please. Keep going in more or less one area of your paper, but if they stray a little it doesn't matter. Don't try to control them, random is the word, just pop them down at random.

Then what happens?

Well, if you're lucky, and you probably will be, after a while you'll look at what you have drawn and you'll get a surprise. You could suddenly see a face staring back at you, or a strange fish, or a camel's nose, or something. I was dotting away once and suddenly saw the head of a lioness quite clearly amongst the dots. Now, if someone had asked me to draw the head of a lioness, I probably couldn't have done it, even though I'm not bad at drawing. I would have had to copy it from a picture. But there it was, as clear as anything—well, I could see it anyway. It's like looking at clouds. You'll soon see faces up there, or elephants, or fat ladies having a bath or something equally preposterous.

Anyway, when the magic happens and you see something good in the dots, you can try and make it even better, by perhaps dotting round it to make it stand out more, or by adding more dots directly to it. Anyway, if all goes well, you'll end up with a piece of artwork worth thousands of pounds and you'll become famous and people will want your autograph or a signed photograph.

If, however, your efforts fail completely, you can always make your drawing into a paper aeroplane because that's recycling and it's good for the environment. You may also break the world record for the number of seconds a paper aeroplane stays in flight and get famous that way.

In the meantime, have a look at some of my drawings which go with the stories and see if you can find hidden faces. How many can you spot in *It's My House* and in *Cabin 502*, for example?"

For more of Glyn's work, check out: www.glyn-matthews.co.uk
Tell him what you think of the drawings in this book, email him at:
glynmatthews@btinternet.com